CRAZY CREATURES OF THE ANIMAL KINGDOM

WHAT DO YOU KNOW ABOUT ANIMAL MIMICRY?

FRANCINE TOPACIO

PowerKiDS press.

New York

Published in 2021 by The Rosen Publishing Group, Inc.
29 East 21st Street, New York, NY 10010

First Edition

Portions of this work were originally authored by Marie Racanelli and published as *Animal Mimics*. All new material in this edition authored by Francine Topacio.

Editor: Kara Murray
Book Design: Tanya Dellaccio

Photo Credits: Cover James David Phenicie/500px Prime/Getty Images; p. 4 Joshua McCullough/Photolibrary/Getty Images; pp. 5, 9 (bottom) JasonOndreicka/iStock/Getty Images; p. 7 Maciej Olszewski/Shutterstock.com; p. 9 (top) Paul Marcellini/Nature Picture Library/Getty Images; p. 11 (top) Marcia Straub/Moment/Getty Images; p. 11 (bottom) Jasius/Moment/Getty Images; p. 13 kikkerdirk/iStock/Getty Images; p. 14 Pong Wira/Shutterstock.com; p. 17 Stephen Frink/Corbis/Getty Images; p. 19 Gail Shotlander/Moment/Getty Images; p. 21 Vladimir Wrangel/Shutterstock.com; p. 22 Valt Ahyppo/Shutterstock.com.

Library of Congress Cataloging-in-Publication Data

Names: Topacio, Francine, author.
Title: What do you know about animal mimicry? / Francine Topacio.
Description: New York : PowerKids Press, [2021] | Series: Crazy creatures of the animal kingdom | Includes index.
Identifiers: LCCN 2019057359 | ISBN 9781725319721 (paperback) | ISBN 9781725319745 (library binding) | ISBN 9781725319738 (6 pack)
Subjects: LCSH: Mimicry (Biology)—Juvenile literature. | Animals—Adaptation—Juvenile literature.
Classification: LCC QH546 .T67 2020 | DDC 591.47/3—dc23
LC record available at https://lccn.loc.gov/2019057359

Manufactured in the United States of America

CPSIA Compliance Information: Batch #CSPK20. For Further Information contact Rosen Publishing, New York, New York at 1-800-237-9932.

CONTENTS

COPYCATS IN NATURE

Think of how many animals live in our world. Some of these animals are **predators**, and some of them will end up as **prey**. They all need to eat. They all need to keep themselves safe. Some animals, over time, have **adapted** to have certain features that match those of other **species**. These adaptations fool their predators and help the animals live longer. These animals are called **mimics**, and the behavior is called mimicry.

Mimics copy the appearance, action, or sound of another animal that predators fear or don't like to eat. The animals they copy are called models. Now let's learn more about these natural copycats!

HOW STRANGE!

Plants can also be mimics. One plant has leaves with yellow spots that mimic the eggs of butterflies that feed on the plant. This tells butterflies to find another place to lay their eggs!

The caterpillar of the spicebush swallowtail butterfly looks like a small snake. The black eyespots and markings on its back end look very much like a snake's head!

KINDS OF MIMICRY

Animal mimicry can take different forms. One kind is called Batesian mimicry. It's named after Henry Walter Bates, a naturalist, or someone who studies the natural world. He discovered that some animals without **defenses** adapted to their **environment** by copying or looking like **dangerous** animals. These weaker animals have no stingers or **poisons** to defend themselves. Instead, they look very much like other animals that do, and so predators leave them alone.

One example of Batesian mimicry is the hoverfly. This fly has adapted to have yellow and black stripes like a bee. Animals know that a bee can sting, so they leave the hoverfly alone.

Would you run away from this insect, thinking it was a bee or wasp? Unlike bees and wasps, though, hoverflies can't sting.

MORE BATESIAN MIMICRY

In Batesian mimicry, it can be hard to tell the defenseless animal from the dangerous one. Coral, king, and milk snakes are excellent examples of Batesian mimicry. Coral snakes are poisonous. King and milk snakes are not. Coral snakes have colorful **scales** in bands of black, red, and yellow. Their yellow bands always touch the red ones. Some king and milk snakes also have bands of red, black, and yellow, but they're arranged in a different order.

It's not always easy to tell these snakes apart. A predator will often stay away from king or milk snakes because it sees their colors and believes they might be poisonous.

HOW STRANGE!

Sometimes Batesian mimicry can mean an animal makes sounds like a more dangerous one! The burrowing owl makes a hissing sound like a rattlesnake to warn predators to stay out of its burrow.

The king snake's coloring is an adaptation that helps keep the snake safe. These snakes have no venom themselves, unlike the highly poisonous coral snake.

STAY AWAY!

Müllerian mimicry is a little different from Batesian mimicry. It's named after Fritz Müller, a German **zoologist**. Müllerian mimicry occurs when animals from two different species look alike and either both are poisonous or one is poisonous and the other tastes bad. Generally, these animals are both brightly colored. The colors are a warning sign to predators that the animals should be left alone.

Monarch and viceroy butterflies are good examples of Müllerian mimicry. The colors and markings on their wings look alike. The monarch is poisonous, though, and the viceroy tastes very bad. A bird that has tried to eat either one will likely just stay away from both.

Viceroy butterflies look like monarchs. The plants viceroys feed on make them taste bitter. This makes birds likely to leave them alone along with the poisonous monarch.

MORE MÜLLERIAN MIMICRY

In Müllerian mimicry, looking alike helps both species since predators think they're the same. There are some places where animals of different species look like each other. These are called rings of Müllerian mimicry. An example of this are poison dart frogs in South America. One species, *Ranitomeya imitator*, has different color patterns depending on where it lives. Each form matches another poisonous species in the area. Predators learn to stay away from all these small frogs with similar bright colors and patterns.

The **indigenous** people who live in the area sometimes use poison dart frogs' **toxins** when they hunt. This is why the frogs are known as poison dart or poison arrow frogs.

HOW STRANGE!

Ranitomeya imitator can look totally different in different places! They can have spots, stripes, orange and black bands, or an unusual orange-and-black body pattern with blue and black legs.

Poison dart frogs come in many brightly colored patterns. The colors let predators know they're poisonous! One version of *Ranitomeya imitator* looks just like this frog.

ALL ABOUT MIMICRY

1 Mimicry might be noticed more in the animal kingdom, but plants can be mimics too!

2 Certain ant-eating spiders mimic ants, making it easier for them to enter an ant colony and attack.

3 Parrots and mockingbirds mimic other bird's songs and sometimes other sounds, such as car alarms or people's voices.

RED ANT MIMIC SPIDER EATING A RED ANT

4 Many mimics are insects, such as butterflies and moths.

5 Self-mimicry occurs when a part of an animal's body looks like another part.

6 Hoverflies, which look like honeybees, have even been known to pretend to sting when attacked!

7 Rhymes help people tell the difference between coral snakes and their mimics. One example is, "If red touches yellow, avoid this fellow."

8 Hawk-moth caterpillars tuck in their heads, bend their bodies, show off their eyespots, and mimic snakes. They even move like snakes! The caterpillars exist for 10 to 30 days but spend only a few days in the snakelike form.

SELF-MIMICRY

Have you ever wondered which end was the head on a caterpillar? Some animals have a type of defense called self-mimicry. These creatures often have body parts that mimic other parts. Often these animals have markings called eyespots.

Self-mimicry isn't used only by prey. Sometimes predators, such as frogmouth catfish, use self-mimicry too. A frogmouth catfish has something on its tongue that looks like food other fish might like to eat. The catfish lies very still, sticking out its long tongue. When a small fish approaches to try to eat the "food," the catfish quickly eats the smaller fish!

HOW STRANGE!

Eyespots have many uses! They may draw a predator's attention to a part of the body that isn't the head. They can also make an animal look larger or scarier.

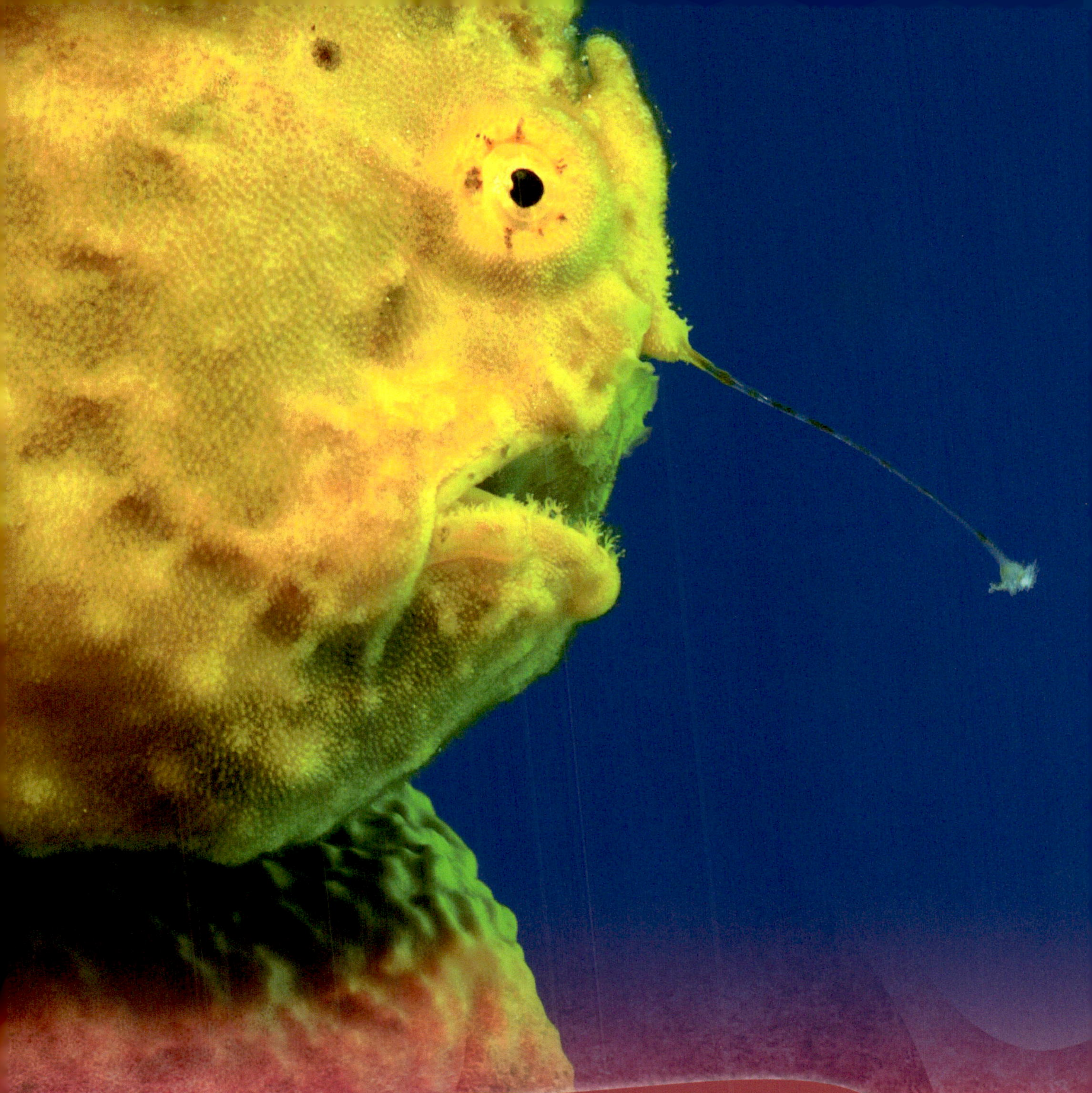

The longlure frogfish is a fish that fishes for its dinner! It has a body part like a lure. It lies in wait and then wiggles its lure to draw prey close.

FALSE EYES

Some butterflies, moths, fish, frogs, and caterpillars have large circles on their bodies. These circles are called eyespots because they look like eyes.

Predators generally like to approach their prey without being seen. Eyespots confuse predators, and they end up coming toward their prey from the wrong side. The prey sees them coming and has time to escape.

Eyespots can keep animals safe in another way too. Some animals, such as Io moths, hawk-moth caterpillars, and false-eyed frogs, have markings that look like the eyes of a bigger animal. These large false eyes scare away predators.

HOW STRANGE!

The northern pygmy owl has spots on the back of its head that look like another pair of eyes!

The owl butterfly has large eyespots on its wings that look like the eyes of an owl. The coloring on its wings might help to fool a predator too.

BODY-PART MIMICS

The animals that can mimic another body part have an important way to keep themselves safe. This form of mimicry helps animals draw attention away from important body parts, such as the head. Predators likely will bite a part of the body that won't hurt the prey as much.

There are some snakes that have tails that look like heads or heads that look like tails. This mimicry saves the snake because a bird trying to eat the snake might not bite the head. The bird also could be tricked and not catch the snake at all if it starts moving in the opposite direction from what the bird expected.

On this copperband butterfly fish, the large eyespot on the back is more noticeable than the small eyes of the fish.

HELPFUL MIMICRY

Mimicry allows animals that have adapted to use it to live longer in their habitats, which is the goal of most animals. Over time, animals that looked like something that scared or confused predators were more likely to live. The animals that didn't have these special colors or markings were less likely to survive.

At the same time, predators have adapted too. They learned which animals might hurt them and started staying away from them. Changing when the environment changes is key to a species' survival over time. Mimicry is just one of the many tools animals have adapted to live in our amazing natural world!

SATANIC LEAF-TAILED GECKO

GLOSSARY

adapt: To change in order to live better in a certain environment.

burrow: A hole an animal digs in the ground for shelter.

dangerous: Not safe.

defense: A feature of a living thing that helps keep it safe.

environment: The conditions that surround a living thing and affect the way it lives.

indigenous: Living naturally in a particular region.

mimic: Something that copies the way other things look, act, or sound.

poison: Something that causes pain or death.

predator: An animal that kills other animals for food.

prey: An animal hunted by other animals for food.

scale: One of the thin, dry pieces of skin that form the outer covering of snakes, lizards, and other reptiles.

species: A group of plants or animals that are all the same kind.

toxin: A type of poison.

zoologist: A person who studies animals.

INDEX

WEBSITES

Due to the changing nature of Internet links, PowerKids Press has developed an online list of websites related to the subject of this book. This site is updated regularly. Please use this link to access the list: www.powerkidslinks.com/ccotak/mimic